I0417929

Making Therapy Work

WORKBOOK & JOURNAL

Exercises and reflections to
make progress in therapy

Kristen Lundquist Mahosky, LPC

THE HEIGHTS
COUNSELING & WELLNESS

Copyright © 2025 by Kristen Lundquist Mahosky

All rights reserved. No part of this publication may be reproduced, stored in a retrieval system, or transmitted in any form or by any means—electronic, mechanical, photocopying, recording, or otherwise—without the prior written permission of the author, except for brief quotations used in reviews or scholarly works. For permissions or inquiries, contact: klundquist@theheightscounseling.com.

Book Title: Making Therapy Work
Author: Kristen Lundquist Mahosky
Editing: Kristen Doerschner
Publisher: The Heights Counseling & Wellness
400 Broad Street, #1006, Sewickley, PA 15143, USA
www.TheHeightsCounseling.com

ISBN: 979-8-218-85699-1 (print)

This book is for educational purposes only. It is not a substitute for professional mental health treatment, diagnosis, or medical advice. Reading this material does not establish a therapeutic relationship with the author. If you are experiencing emotional distress or a mental health emergency, please contact a licensed mental health professional or call your local emergency services immediately. Before you begin working through this book, it is important to consult with your medical doctor and/or mental health provider. They can help you determine if these exercises are a good fit for your current needs and health. Consulting with your medical doctor and/or mental health provider ensures you have the right support in place as you engage in deeper reflection and growth.

To Mom,
Your heart is full of compassion,
and you teach me how to persevere.

CONTENTS

Introduction

As a mental health therapist, I've seen how significant change takes place when people approach their healing with intention. Therapy is more than just talking. It's about setting clear goals, developing useful tools, and taking time out for reflection in order to gain valuable insight. These components create the structure that is needed to move forward with clarity and purpose.

I've created this workbook and journal to help you engage in that process. Inside you will find both exercises and prompts designed to help you set meaningful goals, build effective coping skills, and navigate life's challenges with resiliency. The beautiful thing is that you don't have to be in therapy to benefit from these tools. They are here to support your growth, wherever you are in your journey.

Most importantly, this book invites reflection. Insight is gained as you slow down to process your experiences, find patterns, and connect more deeply with yourself. Each page is an invitation to move forward with intention – equipping and empowering you with what you need to turn insight into meaningful, lasting change.

Whether you are just starting out on your healing journey, or are continuing the work you have already started, this book is here to guide and support you every step of the way.

May you find the utmost healing on your journey!

With gratitude,

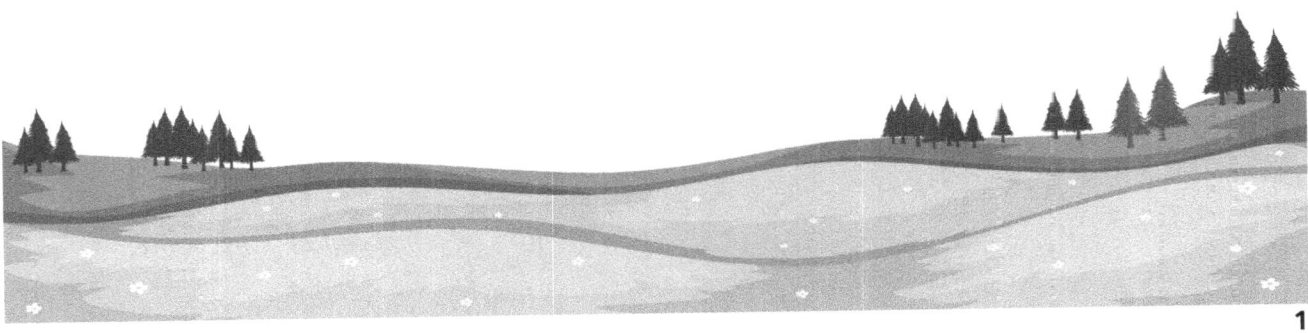

How to Use This Book

Goal Setting: As you begin this workbook and journal, start with the goal setting section. Defined goals provide a map for change, helping you track progress and move forward with clarity and purpose.

Toolkit: Throughout your therapy journey, complete the worksheets in this section to build your emotional resilience, strengthen your relationships, and align your life with what matters most.

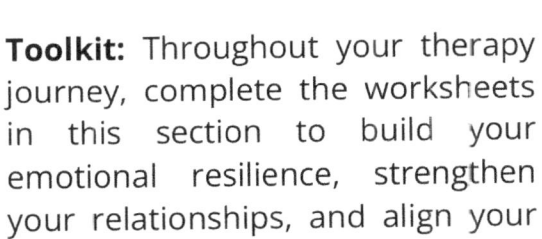

Therapy Journal: Process your sessions and track your progress in therapy by using the journaling pages.

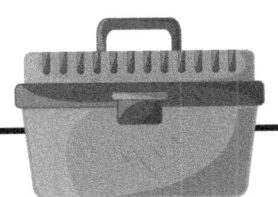

Check your Navigation: Each month, revisit your goals and assess what's working in therapy. Share your insights with your therapist to guide your healing process.

Goal Setting

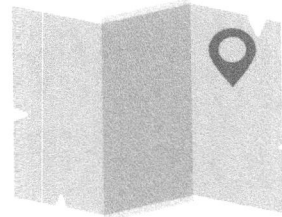

"You can't go back and change the
beginning, but you can start where
you are and change the ending."
-C.S. Lewis

Identifying Your 'Why' in Therapy

As you enter into this reflective and therapeutic process, it is both helpful and vital to fully understand your motivation for entering this healing journey. The things that motivate us become ongoing beacons that can both guide and encourage us through challenging aspects of the process. Take time to answer the following questions to gain a sense of clarity regarding your motivations in this process.

1. What was the experience that motivated you to start your therapy journey?

2. Are there other situations or people that are connected to your journey in therapy? How are they connected to your motivation to pursue healing?

Identifying Your 'Why' in Therapy

3. Considering the context of your therapy journey, what are the areas of your life that are most affected? (Please circle and explain below.)

- Psychological
- Physical
- Emotional
- Professional

- Environmental
- Spiritual
- Financial
- Relational

4. Ultimately, why would pursuing healing in these areas help you?

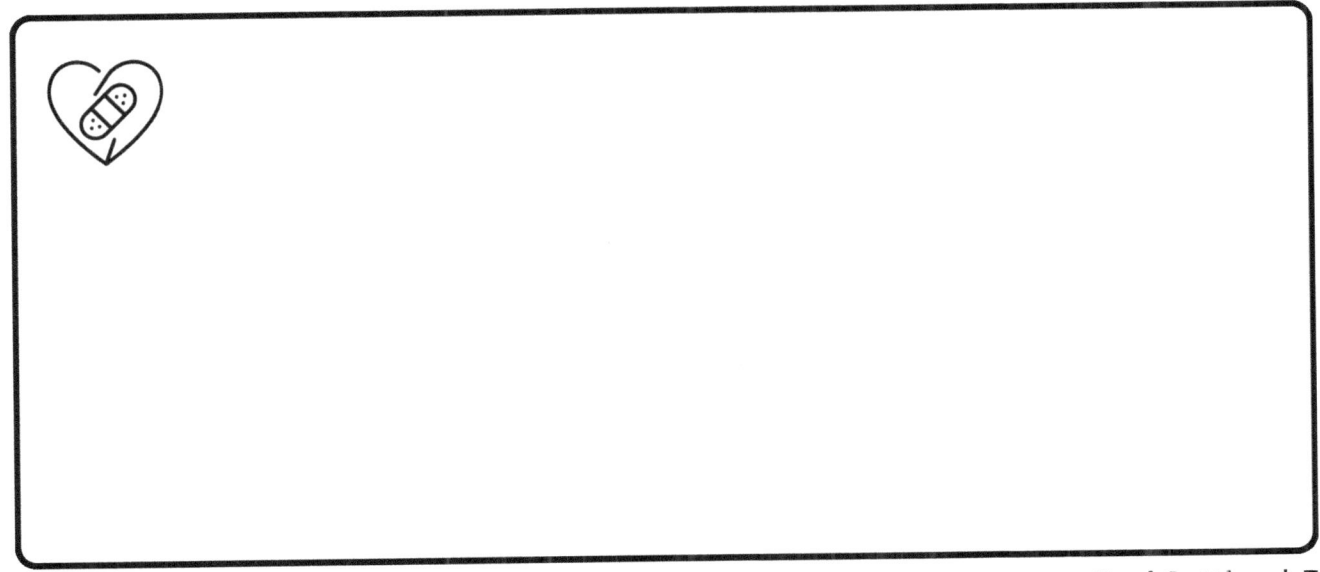

Naming Your Goals

Identifying goals in therapy helps to produce clarity, focus, and direction. Clear goals give measurable benchmarks for our progress, guide the work we do in session, and empower us to take ownership of our healing and growth. Answer the questions below to identify your therapy goals.

1. What would you like to be different in your life at the end of your healing journey?

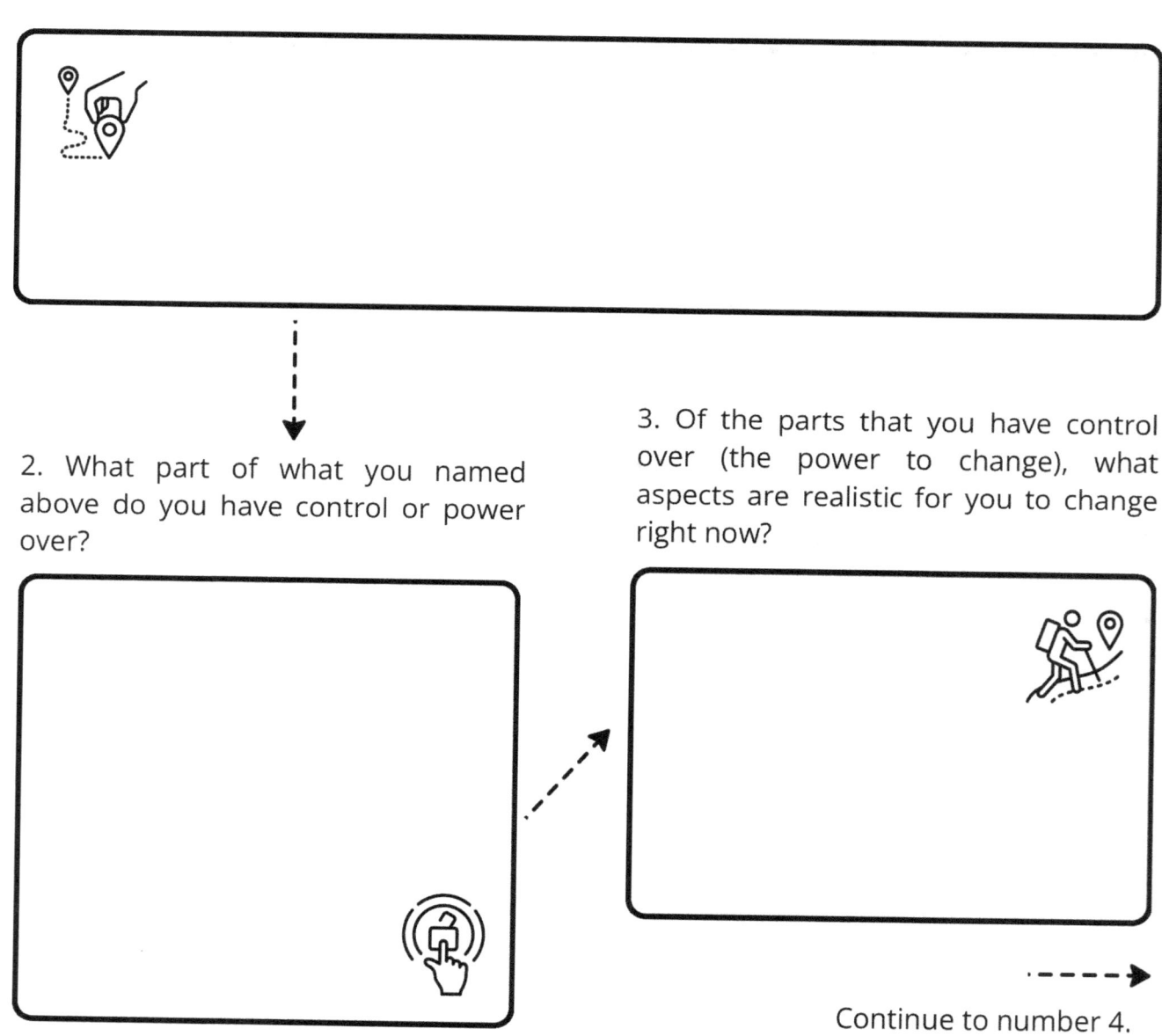

2. What part of what you named above do you have control or power over?

3. Of the parts that you have control over (the power to change), what aspects are realistic for you to change right now?

Continue to number 4.

Naming Your Goals

4. List the changes that are within your control and realistic for you right now (goals). Then below each one, list the smaller day-to-day changes that might indicate that these larger changes are happening. (Example: If the desired change/goal is to pivot to a more fulfilling career, an indicator might be that you are excited to go to work.)

Goal 1:

Indicators:

Goal 2:

Indicators:

Goal 3:

Indicators:

5. As you think about your goals, what are the core fears and desires that you feel? (Example: If your goal is to build a supportive community of friends, a core desire might be acceptance and belonging. A core fear might be rejection and isolation.) Process these desires and fears with your therapist.

Visualizing Your Progress

What will it be like when you see positive change toward your stated goals? Using art supplies (e.g., colored pencils, pens, markers, crayons, etc.) and/or picture cut-outs, create a collage. What do you notice about the themes that appear in your collage? (Example: There are lots of joyful people shown. There are lots of calming colors used.)

Creating a Roadmap for Healing

Goal 1:

Treatment Method(s): After discussing your goal with your therapist, circle the chosen treatment method(s).

- Acceptance and Commitment Therapy (ACT)
- Adlerian Therapy
- Animal-assisted Therapy
- Art Therapy
- Attachment Therapy
- Behavioral Therapy
- Bibliotherapy
- Biofeedback
- Brainspotting
- Brief Psychotherapy
- Clinical Hypnosis
- Cognitive Behavioral Therapy (CBT)
- Compassion-Focused Therapy (CFT)
- Dialectical Behavioral Therapy (DBT)
- Drama Therapy
- Emotionally Focused Therapy (EFT)
- Existential Therapy
- Exposure Therapy
- Eye Movement and Desensitization Therapy (EMDR)
- Family Systems Therapy
- Gestalt Therapy
- Gottman Method Couples Therapy
- Holistic Psychotherapy

- Humanistic Therapy
- Internal Family Systems (IFS)
- Interpersonal Psychotherapy (IPT)
- Logotherapy
- Meaning-centered Psychotherapy
- Mindfulness-based Cognitive Therapy (MBCT)
- Mindfulness-based Stress Reduction (MBSR)
- Music Therapy
- Narrative Therapy
- Neuropsychotherapy
- Person-Centered Therapy (PCT)
- Play Therapy
- Psychedelic-Assisted Psychotherapy (PAP)
- Psychoanalysis
- Psychodynamic Therapy
- Rational Emotive Behavior Therapy (REBT)
- Relational Psychotherapy
- Sensorimotor Therapy
- Solutions-Focused Brief Therapy (SFBT)
- Somatic Experiencing

Additional Treatment Methods:

Creating a Roadmap for Healing

Please review **goal one** after each therapy session and choose a number that reflects how you feel you've progressed toward this goal. The scale runs from 1 to 10 (1 = low progress; 10 = high progress). Circle 'YES' or "NO" to indicate whether the goal has been met. If additional scaling is needed, there are open pages at the end of this book.

1	2	3	4	5	6	7	8	9	10	Complete?	YES / NO
1	2	3	4	5	6	7	8	9	10	Complete?	YES / NO
1	2	3	4	5	6	7	8	9	10	Complete?	YES / NO
1	2	3	4	5	6	7	8	9	10	Complete?	YES / NO
1	2	3	4	5	6	7	8	9	10	Complete?	YES / NO
1	2	3	4	5	6	7	8	9	10	Complete?	YES / NO
1	2	3	4	5	6	7	8	9	10	Complete?	YES / NO
1	2	3	4	5	6	7	8	9	10	Complete?	YES / NO
1	2	3	4	5	6	7	8	9	10	Complete?	YES / NO
1	2	3	4	5	6	7	8	9	10	Complete?	YES / NO

For the aforementioned goal, what treatment methods are working for you? What treatment methods are not? Discuss this with your therapist.

Creating a Roadmap for Healing

Goal 2:

Treatment Method(s): After discussing your goal with your therapist, circle the chosen treatment method(s).

- Acceptance and Commitment Therapy (ACT)
- Adlerian Therapy
- Animal-assisted Therapy
- Art Therapy
- Attachment Therapy
- Behavioral Therapy
- Bibliotherapy
- Biofeedback
- Brainspotting
- Brief Psychotherapy
- Clinical Hypnosis
- Cognitive Behavioral Therapy (CBT)
- Compassion-Focused Therapy (CFT)
- Dialectical Behavioral Therapy (DBT)
- Drama Therapy
- Emotionally Focused Therapy (EFT)
- Existential Therapy
- Exposure Therapy
- Eye Movement and Desensitization Therapy (EMDR)
- Family Systems Therapy
- Gestalt Therapy
- Gottman Method Couples Therapy
- Holistic Psychotherapy

- Humanistic Therapy
- Internal Family Systems (IFS)
- Interpersonal Psychotherapy (IPT)
- Logotherapy
- Meaning-centered Psychotherapy
- Mindfulness-based Cognitive Therapy (MBCT)
- Mindfulness-based Stress Reduction (MBSR)
- Music Therapy
- Narrative Therapy
- Neuropsychotherapy
- Person-Centered Therapy (PCT)
- Play Therapy
- Psychedelic-Assisted Psychotherapy (PAP)
- Psychoanalysis
- Psychodynamic Therapy
- Rational Emotive Behavior Therapy (REBT)
- Relational Psychotherapy
- Sensorimotor Therapy
- Solutions-Focused Brief Therapy (SFBT)
- Somatic Experiencing

Additional Treatment Methods:

Creating a Roadmap for Healing

Please review **goal two** after each therapy session and choose a number that reflects how you feel you've progressed toward this goal. The scale runs from 1 to 10 (1 = low progress; 10 = high progress). Circle 'YES' or "NO' to indicate whether the goal has been met. If additional scaling is needed, there are open pages at the end of this book.

1	2	3	4	5	6	7	8	9	10	Complete?	YES / NO
1	2	3	4	5	6	7	8	9	10	Complete?	YES / NO
1	2	3	4	5	6	7	8	9	10	Complete?	YES / NO
1	2	3	4	5	6	7	8	9	10	Complete?	YES / NC
1	2	3	4	5	6	7	8	9	10	Complete?	YES / NO
1	2	3	4	5	6	7	8	9	10	Complete?	YES / NO
1	2	3	4	5	6	7	8	9	10	Complete?	YES / NO
1	2	3	4	5	6	7	8	9	10	Complete?	YES / NO
1	2	3	4	5	6	7	8	9	10	Complete?	YES / NO
1	2	3	4	5	6	7	8	9	10	Complete?	YES / NO

For the aforementioned goal, what treatment methods are working for you? What treatment methods are not? Discuss this with your therapist.

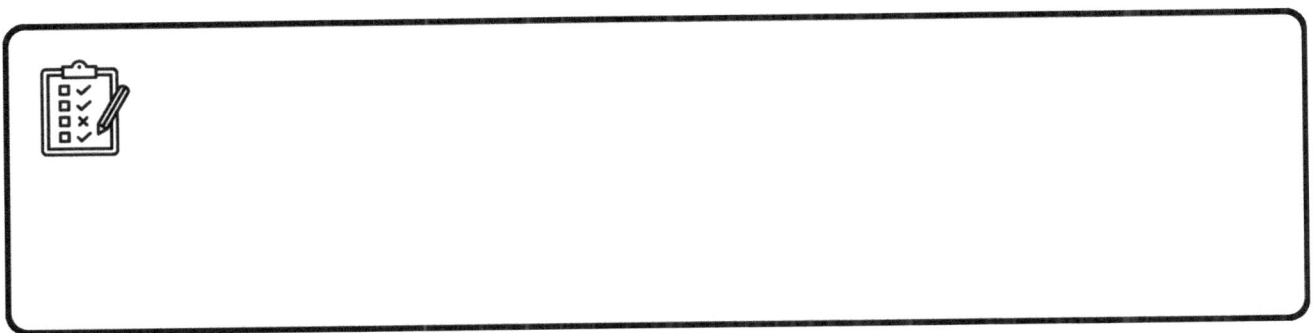

Creating a Roadmap for Healing

Goal 3:

Treatment Method(s): After discussing your goal with your therapist, circle the chosen treatment method(s).

- Acceptance and Commitment Therapy (ACT)
- Adlerian Therapy
- Animal-assisted Therapy
- Art Therapy
- Attachment Therapy
- Behavioral Therapy
- Bibliotherapy
- Biofeedback
- Brainspotting
- Brief Psychotherapy
- Clinical Hypnosis
- Cognitive Behavioral Therapy (CBT)
- Compassion-Focused Therapy (CFT)
- Dialectical Behavioral Therapy (DBT)
- Drama Therapy
- Emotionally Focused Therapy (EFT)
- Existential Therapy
- Exposure Therapy
- Eye Movement and Desensitization Therapy (EMDR)
- Family Systems Therapy
- Gestalt Therapy
- Gottman Method Couples Therapy
- Holistic Psychotherapy

- Humanistic Therapy
- Internal Family Systems (IFS)
- Interpersonal Psychotherapy (IPT)
- Logotherapy
- Meaning-centered Psychotherapy
- Mindfulness-based Cognitive Therapy (MBCT)
- Mindfulness-based Stress Reduction (MBSR)
- Music Therapy
- Narrative Therapy
- Neuropsychotherapy
- Person-Centered Therapy (PCT)
- Play Therapy
- Psychedelic-Assisted Psychotherapy (PAP)
- Psychoanalysis
- Psychodynamic Therapy
- Rational Emotive Behavior Therapy (REBT)
- Relational Psychotherapy
- Sensorimotor Therapy
- Solutions-Focused Brief Therapy (SFBT)
- Somatic Experiencing

Additional Treatment Methods:

Creating a Roadmap for Healing

Please review **goal three** after each therapy session and choose a number that reflects how you feel you've progressed toward this goal. The scale runs from 1 to 10 (1 = low progress; 10 = high progress). Circle 'YES' or "NO" to indicate whether the goal has been met. If additional scaling is needed, there are open pages at the end of this book.

1	2	3	4	5	6	7	8	9	10	Complete?	YES / NO
1	2	3	4	5	6	7	8	9	10	Complete?	YES / NO
1	2	3	4	5	6	7	8	9	10	Complete?	YES / NO
1	2	3	4	5	6	7	8	9	10	Complete?	YES / NO
1	2	3	4	5	6	7	8	9	10	Complete?	YES / NO
1	2	3	4	5	6	7	8	9	10	Complete?	YES / NO
1	2	3	4	5	6	7	8	9	10	Complete?	YES / NO
1	2	3	4	5	6	7	8	9	10	Complete?	YES / NO
1	2	3	4	5	6	7	8	9	10	Complete?	YES / NO
1	2	3	4	5	6	7	8	9	10	Complete?	YES / NO

For the aforementioned goal, what treatment methods are working for you? What treatment methods are not? Discuss this with your therapist.

Toolkit

"The secret of life is to let every segment of it produce its own yield at its own pace. Every period has something new to teach us."
-Sr. Joan D. Chittister

Building Coping Skills

Gaining coping skills during therapy is crucial because it equips and empowers you with practical tools to manage stress and overwhelming emotions. These skills aid you in responding to challenges in healthier and adaptive ways. This supports your progress and provides stability between sessions. By practicing coping skills, you build resiliency and confidence, which allows you to proactively engage in your healing process and foster lasting change in your daily life.

Sit down: This aids in helping the body come out of fight-or-flight.

Deep belly breaths: This helps activate the vagus nerve, which aids in relaxation.

Compassionate touch: This helps comfort the body.

Sing/hum/laugh: This helps activate the vagus nerve.

Loved one: Think of a safe and loved person. Counters stress.

Calming place: Visualize a place where you feel calm.

Look up: This helps take the body out of the tunnel vision of fight-or-flight.

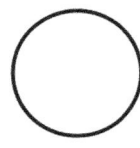

Space: Focus on open space and look up. This moves us from tunnel vision to an open view.

Release: Intentionally relax your muscles.

Move: Give your body a way to process through excess energy.

Reframing Anxious Thoughts

Reframing anxious thoughts helps you see situations with more curiosity and clarity. Instead of getting trapped in worst-case scenarios, you learn to challenge and change unhelpful thoughts into more balanced ones. This shift often reduces anxiety and can provide a greater sense of control in your daily life.

1. If this were happening to someone you love (example: a child), what would you tell them?

2. Zoom out 20 years from now, what might you remember about this experience?

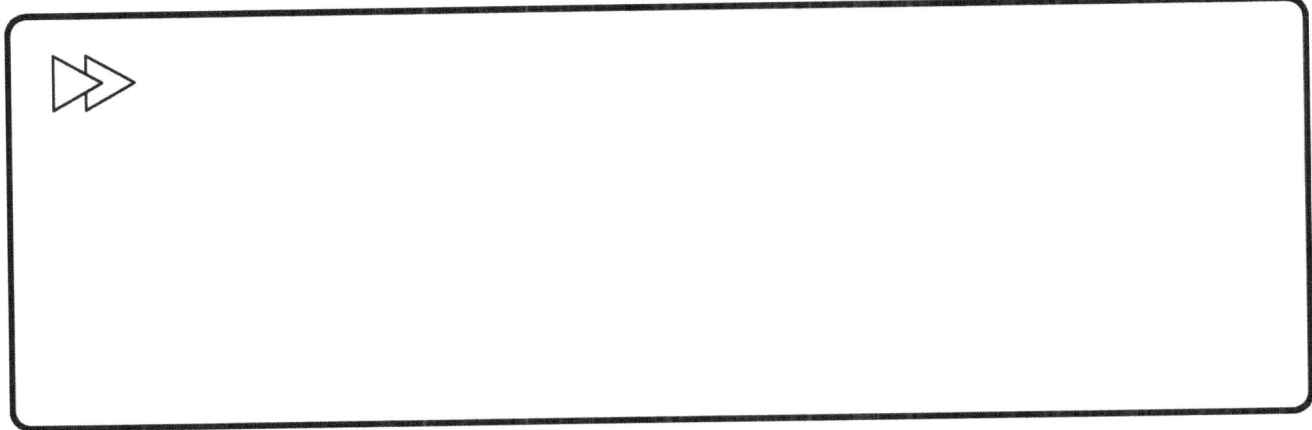

3. Normalize this as a human experience and remember that you are not alone. Has this happened before in history / to others?

4. If you only lay out the facts of the experience (not assumptions or perceptions), what do you notice?

5. Is dwelling on this experience helping? What are three helpful and healthy things you could do to resolve or cope with this experience?

Learning Emotional Language

Examining and naming your emotions is an important step in gaining understanding of self and personal needs. When you can identify what you're feeling it becomes easier to manage your reactions and make decisions that are in alignment with your values. Naming your emotions also helps you communicate more clearly with others, building stronger and healthier connections.

1. Think of something you do multiple times a day (example: wash hands, eat a meal, walk to your car, drink coffee, etc.). During each of these times, ask a simple question: "How am I feeling right now?" Try to find specific language for your experience versus only using simple words like sad, mad, happy (see alternative words below). You might utilize words from the list below.

2. Record your answers using the worksheet on the next page.

3. At the end of every week, look back through your list(s) and get curious about the context in which these emotions occurred. This reflection can potentially provide insight into needed changes and/or needed support.

- Aggressive
- Amazed
- Angry
- Annoyed
- Anxious
- Apathetic
- Ashamed
- Bemused
- Betrayed
- Calm
- Confident
- Confused
- Content

- Delighted
- Disappointed
- Distant
- Disgusted
- Embarrassed
- Empty
- Excited
- Frustrated
- Fulfilled
- Furious
- Grateful
- Guilty
- Happy

- Hesitant
- Hopeful
- Hurt
- Jealous
- Joyful
- Judgmental
- Lonely
- Loving
- Optimistic
- Overwhelmed
- Peaceful
- Proud
- Provoked

- Relaxed
- Resentful
- Revolted
- Sad
- Scared
- Sensitive
- Skeptical
- Stressed
- Surprised
- Terse
- Tranquil
- Violated
- Worried

Learning Emotional Language

SUN	
SAT	
FRI	
THURS	
WEDS	
TUES	
MON	

Noticing the Body

Awareness of mind and body is critical for understanding how your emotions, thoughts, and sensations are interconnected. Tuning into your body and its signals – like tension or fatigue – gives insight into your emotional state and stress levels. The awareness you gain helps you to respond with intention versus reactivity. This supports emotional regulation, anxiety reduction, and a deeper sense of overall well-being.

Once a day, sit or lie down. Take a scan of your body and notice any sensations. Try not to judge, analyze, or hold on to any one sensation. Just allow your mind to scan and notice.

Using different art mediums (e.g., pencils, crayons, paint, etc.), draw these sensations on the outline below. You can use different textures and color to represent different sensations. Outside the image, you can write any emotions that you felt or things that occurred during that particular day.

Before you begin this activity, notice how you are feeling. Does this activity feel challenging or scary? Exciting or confusing? Be sure and process this with your therapist.

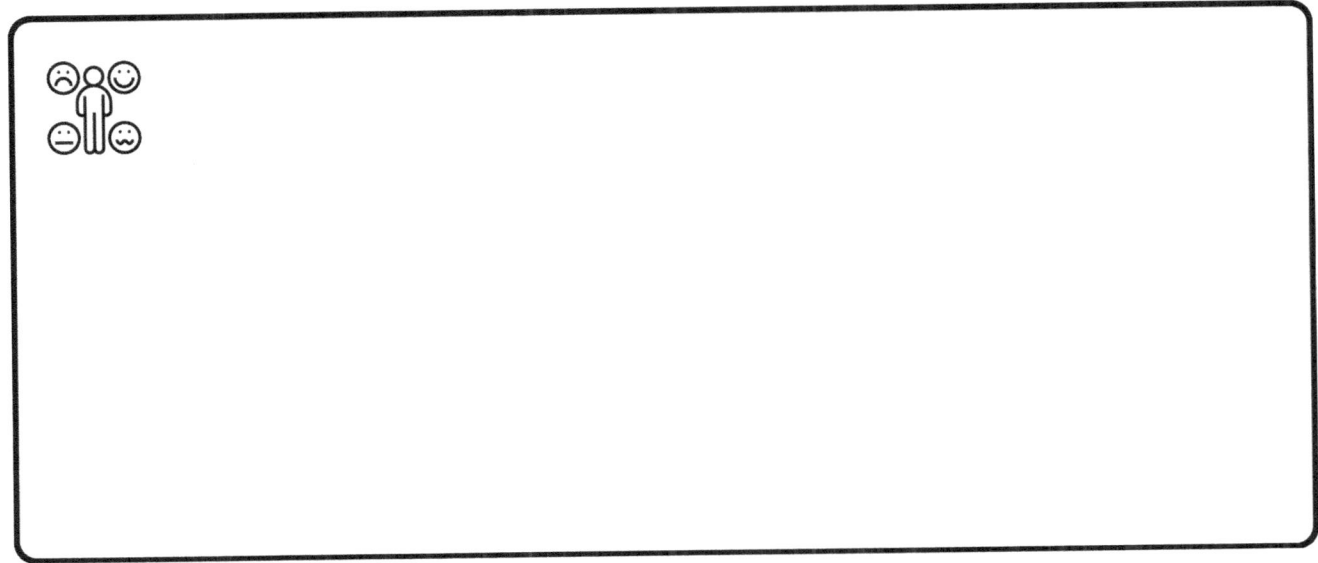

Taking Your Symptom Temperature

Tracking conditions like depression and anxiety is essential for understanding how symptoms change over time and what factors influence them. This information helps individuals and their providers make more informed treatment decisions, adjust coping strategies, and recognize early warning signs of worsening symptoms. Use the chart below to track your chosen symptom throughout the day, noting if it is mild, moderate, or severe.

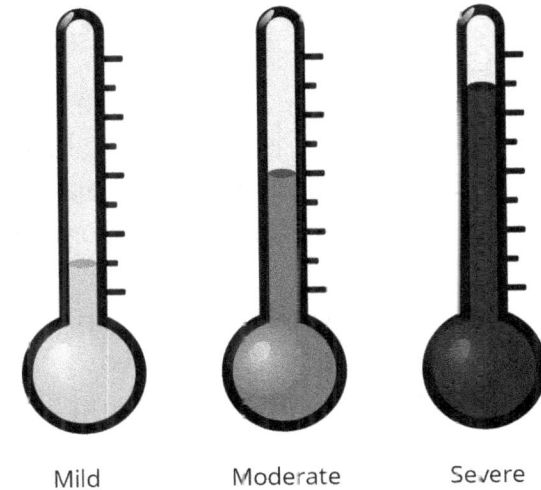

Mild   Moderate   Severe

Symptom: _____   Date Range: _____

	Morning	Mid-Day	Evening
Monday			
Tuesday			
Wednesday			
Thursday			
Friday			
Saturday			
Sunday			

Gaining a Self-compassionate Response

In challenging seasons of life, a self-compassionate response is essential for our emotional resilience and overall well-being. Instead of the harsh criticism we often give ourselves, offer yourself kindness and understanding. This creates a space for growth to occur and reduces shame so we can further regulate any overwhelming emotions.

Responding with compassion allows you to both acknowledge the pain non-judgmentally, and respond with care, much like we would for a loved one. This gentle approach promotes healing and builds inner strength, even in the midst of difficulty.

Step One: Setting the Intention of Presence

- Be with yourself. When hard times hit and you notice your critical voice grabbing the "mental microphone" – stop what you're doing, and observe how you're feeling (physically and emotionally) without judgment.

- Give yourself freedom to just "be," and allow yourself to connect with both your physical body and emotions.

Step Two: Practicing Active Listening

- Allow your thoughts to flow. Pay attention to what comes out – the good, the bad, and the ugly – and instead of responding with commentary or judgment, seek understanding and get curious about the core fears and desires that are in your thoughts.

Gaining a Self-compassionate Response

Step Three: Practicing Affirmation

- When you experience a struggle and the difficult emotions that come with it, it helps to normalize what's happening.

- "This is really tough." "It's natural to be sad during such a loss." Statements like these affirm and validate that what you're experiencing is difficult. It serves to honor your struggle and acknowledge the challenge you are walking through.

- When we respect our experience and normalize our struggle this can be the beginning of combating shame, fear, and loneliness.

Step Four: Practicing the Act of Giving Comfort

- Think of one touch that you've received in your life that has been comforting. Perhaps it was the embrace of a loved one, a shoulder massage, the gentle cupping of a face, or a hand over a heart. Whatever the touch, replicate that for yourself. Place your hand over your heart or gently touch your face while you practice self-affirmation. It's a simple way of reassuring your mind, soul, and body that you are a friend and not a foe.

Gaining a Self-compassionate Response

Step Five: Practicing Healthy Encouragement

- When all is said and done, we want to build up ourselves and move forward. By practicing healthy encouragement with ourselves, we gain strength and motivation to keep going.

- Adopt mantras of: "I am capable of moving forward into new opportunities", "It's okay to ask for help during challenging times", or "I've gained wisdom from this experience that now allows me to help others."

Step Six: Choosing Healthy Behaviors

- Consider three actions (or inactions) that you can adopt that would move you in a healthier direction during this challenging time. It may be related directly to the challenge at hand, or it may simply be behaviors that care for your whole self.

What do you want to remember regarding your self-compassion experience?

Processing Life Experiences

Processing life experiences is vital for emotional growth and overall well-being. Taking time to reflect on the things we go through—both painful and meaningful—can bring clarity, insight, and healing. Experiences that we don't process can linger and haunt us, influencing our thoughts, behaviors, and relationships in ways we may not understand. With intentional processing, we create space for deeper self-awareness and resiliency.

Step One: What occurred? Write it out step-by-step.

- What was my experience?
- What are the details that stand out?
- What are the things I want to emphasize?
- What are the things I want to minimize?

Processing Life Experiences

Step Two: How did/does this experience make you feel?

- How did/does it feel emotionally?
- How did/does it feel physically? (i.e. Where are you feeling it in your body?)

Step Three: What did/does this occurrence mean to you?

- What is the meaning / message I'm absorbing from this occurrence?
- What are the implications of this meaning / message?

Processing Life Experiences

Step Four: What is the self-compassionate response?

- How can I normalize, affirm, and emphathize with myself? (e.g., '____ is a human emotion.' 'It's normal to feel ____.' 'I am worthy of ____.'

Grieving

The process of grieving is a crucial aspect of healing after loss. Grief allows us to honor what we have lost, process how we feel, and gently adjust to a new reality. Without grief, our pain can exist unresolved, and negatively impact our well-being over time. Healthy and intentional grieving provides a way forward, so we don't become frozen in the trauma of our loss.

Step One: Remembering the thing that was....

- What was my experience before this happened? How did this feel?
- What will you miss? (e.g., What were the things that were positive? Stable? Life-giving?)

Grieving

Step Two: Acknowledging the things that will no longer be...

- How will life be different now?
- How does it feel to live in that reality?

Grieving

- What are aspects of the thing(s) that you need to let go of?
- What do you not want to 'haunt' you? Or live on as a 'ghost' in your life?

Grieving

Step Four: Adopting the legacy...

- What are aspects of the thing(s) that you would like to keep alive throughout your life?

Identifying Your Personal Values

Naming your values aids you in understanding what truly matters to you, and provides clarity and direction for your life choices. When your choices align with your core values, a sense of fulfillment, grounding, and authenticity often follow. When you know your values, you can set meaningful goals, make critical decisions, and navigate challenging times, all with a sense of confidence and integrity.

1. To identify your personal values, look through the list on the next page and circle the first ten values that appeal to you.
2. Order your chosen values from most important to least important (1-10).
3. Go through each value and define what it means to you, providing tangible examples of this value (e.g., associated people, experiences, sensations, objects, etc.).
4. Next, consider what five values you would keep if you had to split the list in half. Order the five remaining values from most important to least important (1-5).
5. Take a break from the values list for 24 hours. In that time, observe how these five values factor into your day. Notice what happens within you emotionally when these values are either affirmed or challenged.
6. Finally, consider this metaphor to identify your top two personal values: If a house was on fire and these five values were inside, which two would you choose to 'save' and take with you throughout your life? Order these values in terms of importance (#1 & #2).

Identifying Your Personal Values

- Acceptance
- Accountability
- Adventure
- Ambition
- Appreciation
- Assertiveness
- Authenticity
- Balance
- Beauty
- Belonging
- Bravery
- Calmness
- Care
- Challenge
- Charity
- Clarity
- Collaboration
- Commitment
- Community
- Compassion
- Competence
- Confidence
- Connection
- Consciousness
- Consistency
- Contentment
- Contribution
- Cooperation
- Courage
- Creativity
- Curiosity
- Dignity
- Discipline
- Discovery
- Diversity
- Drive
- Education

- Efficiency
- Empathy
- Endurance
- Equality
- Excellence
- Fairness
- Faith
- Family
- Flexibility
- Focus
- Forgiveness
- Fortitude
- Freedom
- Friendship
- Fun
- Generosity
- Grace
- Growth
- Happiness
- Harmony
- Health
- Honesty
- Honor
- Hope
- Hospitality
- Humility
- Humor
- Independence
- Influence
- Insight
- Integrity
- Intelligence
- Joy
- Justice
- Kindness
- Knowledge
- Leadership

- Learning
- Liberty
- Logic
- Longevity
- Love
- Loyalty
- Meaning
- Mentorship
- Mercy
- Mindfulness
- Moderation
- Modesty
- Motivation
- Morality
- Mutuality
- Nature
- Obedience
- Objectivity
- Openness
- Order
- Organization
- Originality
- Passion
- Patience
- Peace
- Perseverance
- Power
- Presence
- Pride
- Purpose
- Reliability
- Relationships
- Respect
- Reverence
- Rigor
- Safety
- Self-care

- Self-discipline
- Sensitivity
- Service
- Simplicity
- Spirituality
- Stability
- Strength
- Success
- Support
- Sustainability
- Teamwork
- Tenacity
- Tolerance
- Tradition
- Trust
- Truth
- Understanding
- Unity
- Vision
- Vulnerability
- Warmth
- Wealth
- Wholeness
- Wisdom
- Zeal
- Zen

Others:

Identifying Your Personal Values

Values		Definition
1	→	
2	→	
3	→	
4	→	
5	→	
6	→	
7	→	
8	→	
9	→	
10	→	

Identifying Your Personal Values

Top 5 Values

Top 2 Values

Exploring Your Meaning & Purpose

Discovering your personal meaning and purpose can give direction, motivation, and deeper fulfillment. It can help you understand what it is that truly matters to you and guide you in your decision-making. When you live with purpose, challenges can feel more manageable because you are grounded in a sense of why your life and work matter.

1. What are actions that you perceive to be significant (things that matter)?

2. What are your natural passions in life?

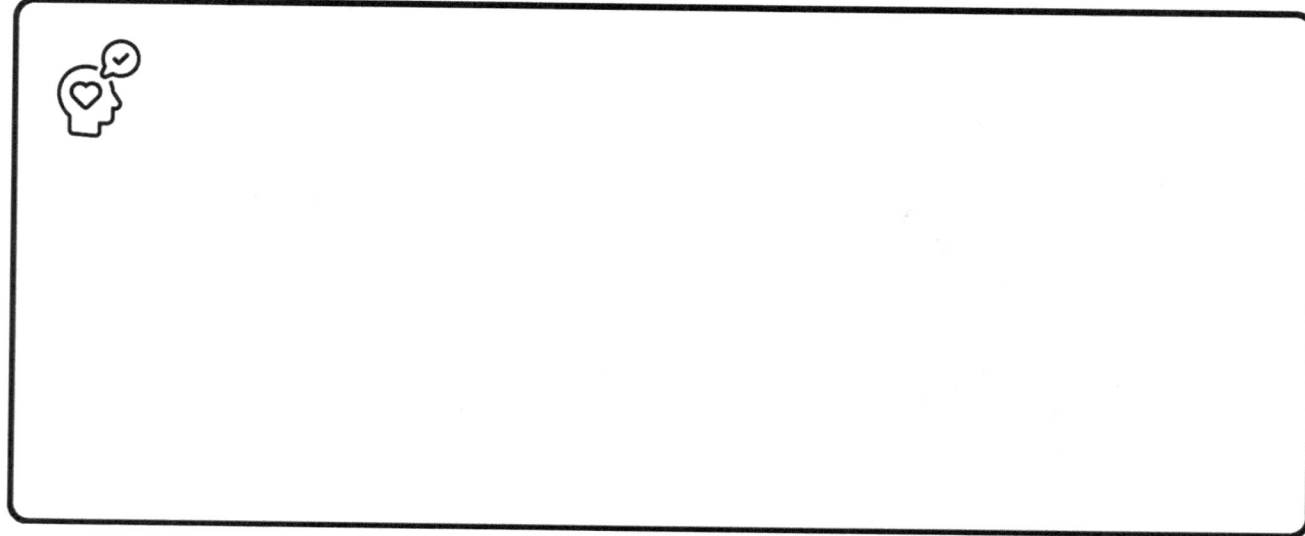

Exploring Your Meaning & Purpose

3. What are the relationships and connections that bring a sense of direction or meaning to life?

4. What are the things in your life that bring a sense of coherence, order, regularity?

5. What is the 'why' behind the actions you take on a daily basis?

Discovering Your Personal Identity

Identity examination and formation are key elements of building resilience. These help you understand who you are, what you value, and what you stand for as an individual. When your identity is strong, you have a foundation and stability during turbulent times and can draw on your strength when situations feel uncertain.

1. What are the defining experiences or memories in my life that have impacted who I am? How?

2. What are the relationships, either past or present, that have impacted who I am? How?

Discovering Your Personal Identity

3. What are the lessons I've taken with me or the legacies of my life experiences and relationships?

4. What are my qualities or personality traits? (Include both bad and good.)

5. What can I affirm about myself? How can I empathize with myself?

Creating Focus and Structure

Building focus and structure into your day supports your mental health through the reduction of overwhelm and the creation of stability. Aligning your routine with your values adds meaning and balance. Dedicating time to nurture relationships helps you stay connected and feel a sense of belonging.

1. What are your core values? (e.g., honesty, success, family, etc.) If there are things in your day that conflict with these values, re-think your long-term commitment to these actions.

2. Who are the most important people in your life? Schedule time daily to connect (vocally or face-to-face) with at least one of these people. Name the person specifically on your schedule.

3. Fill in the blank: *I avoid tasks that make me feel _____.* What are those tasks? Schedule these tasks before noon each day. If possible, do these tasks outside of the home (e.g., office, coffee shop, library, etc.)

Creating Focus and Structure

4. What actions/logistics/tasks are necessary during your week? (e.g., groceries, laundry, gas, etc.) Schedule these tasks right after your 'avoidance' tasks. Typically mid-day.

5. What excites you regarding your current or potential vocation/career/job? Schedule 2-3 times per week to do vision casting. *What do I want to do/create? What problem would I like to address? What would I like to learn that would get me closer to this goal? How does this connect up with my core values?*

6. What time of day do you feel the most negative energy? Schedule 15-minute mindfulness moments where you connect with your emotions and body. *How am I feeling? What does my body feel like?* Apply simple affirming mantras, breathing exercises, and/or progressive muscle relaxation.

Creating Focus and Structure

MONDAY

Top Core Values:

Person I am contacting today (time?):

Vision Casting Day? YES / NO

Highlight challenging parts of the day. Schedule in 15 minutes of mindfulness.

Early Morning:

Mid Morning:

Avoidance Tasks:

Necessary Tasks/Errands:

MID-DAY

Afternoon:

Evening:

Creating Focus and Structure

Tuesday

Top Core Values:

Person I am contacting today (time?):

Vision Casting Day? YES / NO

Highlight challenging parts of the day. Schedule in 15 minutes of mindfulness.

Early Morning:

Mid Morning:

Avoidance Tasks:

Necessary Tasks/Errands:

MID-DAY

Afternoon:

Evening:

Creating Focus and Structure

Wednesday

Top Core Values:

Person I am contacting today (time?):

Vision Casting Day? YES / NO

Highlight challenging parts of the day. Schedule in 15 minutes of mindfulness.

Early Morning:

Mid Morning:

Avoidance Tasks:

Necessary Tasks/Errands:

MID-DAY

Afternoon:

Evening:

Creating Focus and Structure

Thursday

Top Core Values:

Person I am contacting today (time?):

Vision Casting Day? YES / NO

Highlight challenging parts of the day. Schedule in 15 minutes of mindfulness.

Early Morning:

Mid Morning:

Avoidance Tasks:

Necessary Tasks/Errands:

MID-DAY

Afternoon:

Evening:

Creating Focus and Structure

Friday

Top Core Values:

Person I am contacting today (time?):

Vision Casting Day? YES / NO

Highlight challenging parts of the day. Schedule in 15 minutes of mindfulness.

Early Morning:

Mid Morning:

Avoidance Tasks:

Necessary Tasks/Errands:

MID-DAY

Afternoon:

Evening:

Creating Focus and Structure

Saturday

Top Core Values:

Person I am contacting today (time?):

Vision Casting Day? YES / NO

✎ **Highlight challenging parts of the day. Schedule in 15 minutes of mindfulness.**

Early Morning:

Mid Morning:

Avoidance Tasks:

Necessary Tasks/Errands:

MID-DAY

Afternoon:

Evening:

Creating Focus and Structure

Sunday

Top Core Values: [ ]

Person I am contacting today (time?): [ ]

Vision Casting Day? [YES / NO]

✏️ **Highlight challenging parts of the day. Schedule in 15 minutes of mindfulness.**

Early Morning: [ ]

Mid Morning: [ ]

Avoidance Tasks: [ ]

Necessary Tasks/Errands: [ ]

MID-DAY

Afternoon: [ ]

Evening: [ ]

Accessing Your Agency

Examining your own agency brings a sense of empowerment and reminds you that you have influence over your daily choices and responses. In recognizing your ability to respond and act with intention, you cultivate feelings of control and stability, which support resiliency and emotional balance even in the midst of turbulent times.

Control the Input

- What information am I consuming?
- How can I avoid overstimulation?

Move & Be in Nature

- What type of movement is my body lacking?
- When was the last time I connected with the natural world around me?

Notice Associations

- Who are the people I'm spending most of my time around?
- What are the groups/platforms that I engage with?
- How are these associations affecting me?

Choose Your Fuel

- What are the foods that positively and negatively affect my mood and outlook?

Accessing Your Agency

Commit to Life-long Learning

- What information am I consuming?
- How can I avoid overstimulation?

Reflect then Act

- Have I taken ample time to process and consider this issue / topic?
- If so, how can I act and make a positive difference (no matter how small)?

Be Aware of Emotions & Blocking Beliefs

- How do my beliefs, emotions, and perspectives influence my behavior?
- Do any of them create unnecessary obstacles?

Offer Up & Let Go

- What is beyond my influence?
- What do I need to offer up to a higher power or influence?
- What do I need to grieve and release?

Notice Your Intuition

- Am I responding out of a gut reaction? Out of a strategic position? Or based on expert knowledge?

Other:

Learning Good Communication and Assertiveness in Conflict

Good communication and assertiveness help you approach and resolve conflict by expressing your needs clearly and respectfully. This prevents misunderstandings, fosters healthy boundary setting, and enables mutual trust.

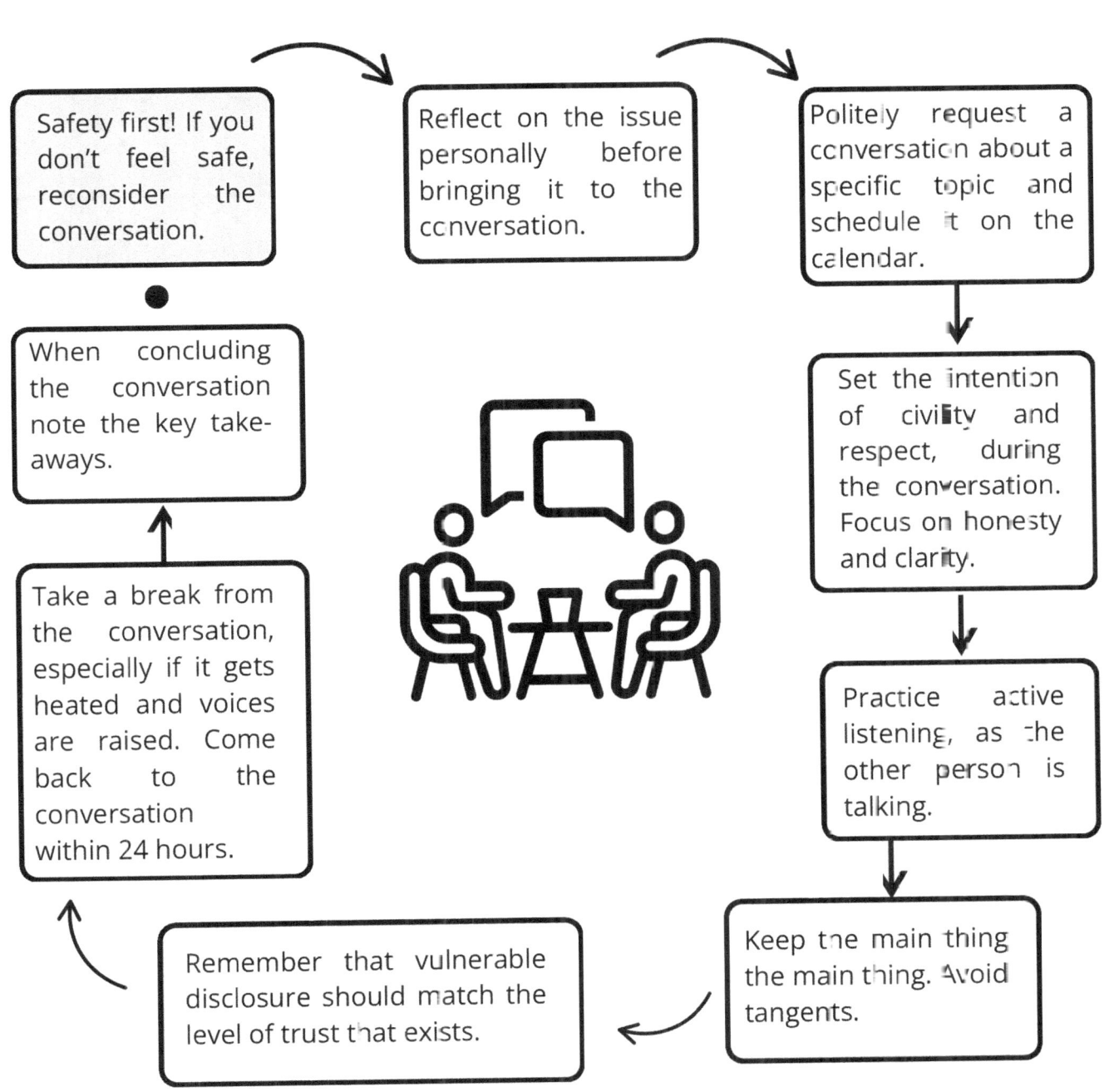

Safety first! If you don't feel safe, reconsider the conversation.

Reflect on the issue personally before bringing it to the conversation.

Politely request a conversation about a specific topic and schedule it on the calendar.

When concluding the conversation note the key take-aways.

Set the intention of civility and respect, during the conversation. Focus on honesty and clarity.

Take a break from the conversation, especially if it gets heated and voices are raised. Come back to the conversation within 24 hours.

Practice active listening, as the other person is talking.

Remember that vulnerable disclosure should match the level of trust that exists.

Keep the main thing the main thing. Avoid tangents.

Transforming Loneliness through Community Building

Fostering healthy and balanced community is essential for mental health because it provides a sense of belonging, support, and connection that combats loneliness. Meaningful relationships create space to share your experiences, give and receive encouragement, and foster feelings of understanding. This can reduce a sense of isolation and improve well-being. Strong social supports contribute to our resilience and offer practical and emotional care during challenging times. Community often reminds us that we are not alone in our struggles.

1. Internal before External

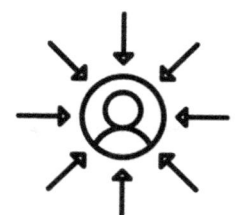

- What do you appreciate about yourself?
- What do you value?
- What brings you delight?
- What challenges are you trying to address?
- What issues or topics do you feel passionate about?
- Write the answers to these questions below.

2. Deepen what Exists

- Look around at the relationships you have. Which relationships have the possibility of deepening trust?
- Which relationships feel positive and balanced? Write these below.
- Initiate one-on-one meetups to see if there is potential to go deeper in relationship.

3. Do Your Homework

- Using keywords, search for groups in your area that align with your values, passions, interests, and/or personality. Write these groups below.

4. Start Small

- Choose one group or person with which to engage. Too many people or groups can be overwhelming. Write the group or person below.

5. Make a Plan & Engage

- Schedule a meetup with a person or plan to attend a group (sign-up/register). Write the day/time of the group or meetup below.
- Put this on your calendar.
- Set reminders.

6. Manage Your Energy

- Make sure you are well rested, fed, and hydrated prior to meeting up.
- Prepare what you will wear and your transportation in advance.
- Write your checklist below.

7. Try and Try Again

- Remember that close friendships or group connection doesn't happen right away. It can take several times of meeting for this to occur. Try to meet with the same group at least nine times, ideally on a weekly basis.
- Sometimes people don't click or groups don't resonate. This is okay. There are other people and groups.

Fostering Relational Balance and Healthy Boundaries

Relational balance and healthy boundaries are critical for sustaining emotional well-being and respect within relationships. When you communicate your needs, understand others' needs, and set clear limits, you protect your energy, avoid resentment, and foster a safe space for connection. When you set boundaries, you define where you end and others begin. This allows you to stay grounded, keep in alignment with your values, and build relationships of trust. Remember, good boundaries are good for everyone! (Note: physical and/or emotional abuse is never okay. Please seek professional aid and protective services, if you are in this situation.)

Answer the questions below regarding your relationship of focus. Let it aid you in understanding if more relational balance and healthy boundaries are needed (e.g., more answers of 'No' or 'Maybe').

1. Are both you and the other person known, seen, and heard?

Yes ☐   No ☐   Maybe ☐

2. When you consider the other person's requests, are you able to reflect on why and how this makes sense for you?

Yes ☐   No ☐   Maybe ☐

3. When your partner makes a request, is your 'no' respected?

Yes ☐   No ☐   Maybe ☐

4. Is vulnerability respected and honored? Can you be authentic without getting shamed?

Yes ☐   No ☐   Maybe ☐

Fostering Relational Balance and Healthy Boundaries

5. Is there room for voicing and addressing conflict in an assertive way (rather than passive or aggressive)?

Yes ☐   No ☐   Maybe ☐

6. Is there responsiveness and mutual support between you and the other person?

Yes ☐   No ☐   Maybe ☐

7. Do you feel a positive connection with the other person (versus tolerance or disgust)?

Yes ☐   No ☐   Maybe ☐

8. Do you feel empowered by the relationship?

Yes ☐   No ☐   Maybe ☐

9. If the relationship dissolves, do you feel you could maintain your sense of self-worth?

Yes ☐   No ☐   Maybe ☐

10. Is there a sufficient level of trust between you and the other person?

Yes ☐   No ☐   Maybe ☐

Ways to Foster Relational Balance

Respect

- Recognizing your own needs and core values as well as honoring the needs and values of the other person.

Boundaries

- Protecting the emotional safety and trust of the relationship by setting and holding healthy limits.

Personal Identity

- Each person is able to maintain their own goals, interests, pursuits, and friends outside of the relationship.

Mutual Support

- Working to ensure that each person in the relationship gives and receives meaningful support.

Decision-making

- Making decisions together and addressing challenges as a team. Respecting the other person's voice.

Ways to Foster Relational Balance

Communication

- Actively listen with empathy. Keep the discussion about the main thing. Speak clearly and honestly. Take breaks when necessary.

Trust

- Follow through on your commitments to one another, and communicate proactively when you cannot.

Flexibility

- Learning to adjust to the changes of life, without breaking connection.

Presence

- Making yourself available to one another for emotional support, empathy, and encouragement.

Growth

- Supporting one another's development, both personally and relationally.

Ways to Foster Relational Balance

Go internal before external

- Take time to reflect on how the other person's actions affected you. If a boundary is needed, your internal reflection will help you affirm why the boundary is so important and aid you in thoughtfully communicating this to the other person.

Proactive Communication

- Communicate boundaries in advance; don't wait until the next conflict.
- "When you do _____, I feel _____, because of _____. I am requesting that you do _____ instead. If you choose not to honor my request, I will choose to _____."

Awareness

- Be aware that people may get defensive when you communicate a boundary.
- They may use phrases like "Well, you always do _____" or "I can't believe you're making a big deal out of this!" or "You're being too sensitive!"
- Utilize your skills of self-compassionate response, and hold your boundary!

Remember, healthy boundaries create a safe context for relationships of trust to grow. They are healthy for everyone!

Cultivating Gratitude

It can be difficult to focus on the abundance in our lives, especially if we are struggling with depression, anxiety, grief, and/or trauma. This happens for a number of reasons: 1) The body may have an imbalance of 'feel good' chemicals like serotonin and dopamine. This makes it hard to find anything in life enjoyable. 2) The brain may be triggered into the Default Mode Network more often, which allows for negative rumination, especially as focused on the self. 3) Once negative neural pathways (train of thought) are formed, they are reinforced by repetition. This makes it more difficult to change your perspective and ways of thinking.

The good news is that brain change and growth is possible! Focusing on abundance and gratitude encourages the body to be in a relaxed state (rest and digest). Being in a relaxed state allows you to access more positive thought engagement (e.g., curiosity, creativity, etc.). At first it may feel like you are just 'going through the motions' (this may not feel impactful at first). Keep going! With time, you can begin to break down old negative thought patterns and create neural networks that take you in a more positive direction!

 **Quiet Space:** Pause the other things that you are doing, and find a quiet place to sit. Begin taking some deep belly breaths, then notice and relax the tension in your body.

The Basics: Think of 3-5 basic things that you have access to in order to care for yourself (e.g., clean water to drink, a roof to keep you dry from the rain, clothes to protect you from the sun or cold). Write them down. Briefly imagine life without these things, then bring yourself back to the present, take a deep breath, look up (occipital lobe activation), and enjoy the fact that you do have them now. If your mind brings up negative possibilities ('Yeah, but for how much longer will you have them?!') bring it back to what is real right now. The only thing that exists is the present moment.

Cultivating Gratitude

Interactions: Relationships can be complicated, and it can be tempting to only focus on the negative aspects. Bring to mind 2-3 people with whom you have had a respectful and/or positive interaction in the past week. This could be the cashier at the grocery store who said 'Hi', the neighbor who slightly smiled while you walked past, or the friend who sent you a funny meme. Notice that they could have not done these respectful/positive things, or they could have chosen to give a negative reaction. Focus on their positive interaction, however small; and, enjoy the fact that the respect and positivity was directed toward you.

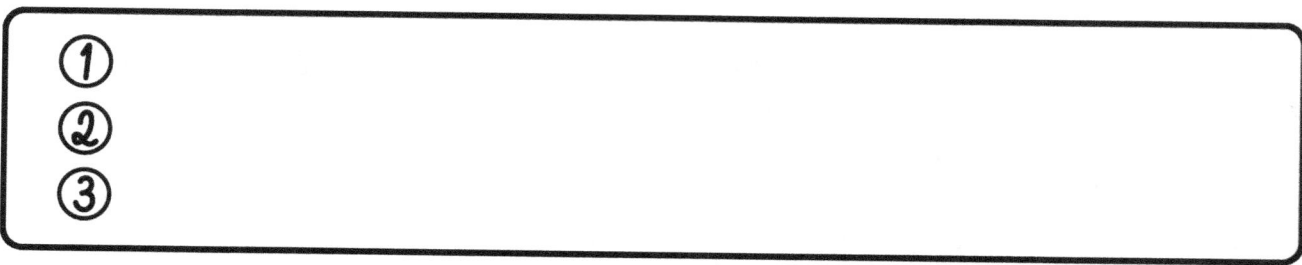

Other Experiences or Items of Abundance: Once you have practiced the aforementioned gratitude meditations for awhile, begin to expand your gratitude practice. Every time you have a meal or snack, begin to think of 2-3 points of abundance in your life (e.g., my dog is always happy to see me; the sun is beautiful shining through my window in the morning, etc.).

Be aware if your mind tries to cancel these things out ('yeah, but...'), take some deep belly breaths, look up (occipital lobe activation), then shift back to focusing on the positive.

Self-care

Self-care is a holistic way to pursue healing. It nurtures our mind, body, and spirit and recognizes that sustainable well-being only comes from caring for all aspects of our being. Self-care is more than occasional rest or enjoyment, but rather is a consistent practice of acknowledging and honoring our physical needs, addressing our emotional health, cultivating supportive community, and fostering a sense of meaning and purpose. True self-care strengthens our resilience, fosters balance, and supports healing in the midst of life's challenges.

Potential Indicators of Burnout (Lack of Self-care):

- Irritability
- Apathy
- Cynicism
- Unhealthy diet
- Increased anxiety
- Existential crisis
- Lack of motivation

- Feeling overwhelmed
- Feeling disconnected or isolated
- Insomnia

- Feelings of helplessness
- Victim mentality
- Physical symptoms

Common Misconceptions of Self-care:

Selfish

Lazy

Lacking Focus

Big Ego

Types of Self-care

Physical

- Utilize gentle movement to keep your body active and healthy.

Emotional

- Take time to process how your experiences make you feel, and respond with self-compassion.

Psychological

- Stop and consider what your experiences mean to you, and evaluate if a change in perspective is needed.

Professional

- Assess your level of work/life balance. What are needed (albeit possibly difficult) changes that need to be made?

Environmental

- Consider if there are aspects of your environment that are negatively affecting your health (e.g. air quality, water purity, etc.). What are possible changes that can be made to move you toward greater health?

Self-care

Spiritual & Cultural

- Reflect on aspects of your cultural heritage or spiritual life with which you can reconnect. What are the practices that bring abundance, balance, healing, and joy?

Financial

- Examine the level of stress your financial situation places on you. If high or moderate, consider working through a financial wellness workbook or money management guide.

Self-care Next Steps:

Type of self-care	Start date	Frequency

Examining Future Decisions

The act of intentional decision making is an important element of mental health. When we allow future decisions to 'haunt' us, we can fall prey to frequent stress and anxiety. Approaching decision making with boundaries, thoughtfulness, and structure keeps us grounded and empowers us to make healthy decisions consistent with our priorities and values.

Elements to Consider in Decision Making:

1. Safe / Legal

- Discern whether the choice keeps you and others safe from harm and is legal.

2. Basic Needs

- Discern whether the choice protects your basic needs (e.g., food, shelter, etc.)

3. Employment / Income

- Discern whether the choice protects your income and/or source of income.

4. Relationships

- Discern whether the choice protects healthy relationships in your life.

5. Values

- Discern whether the choice aligns with your core values.

Examining Future Decisions

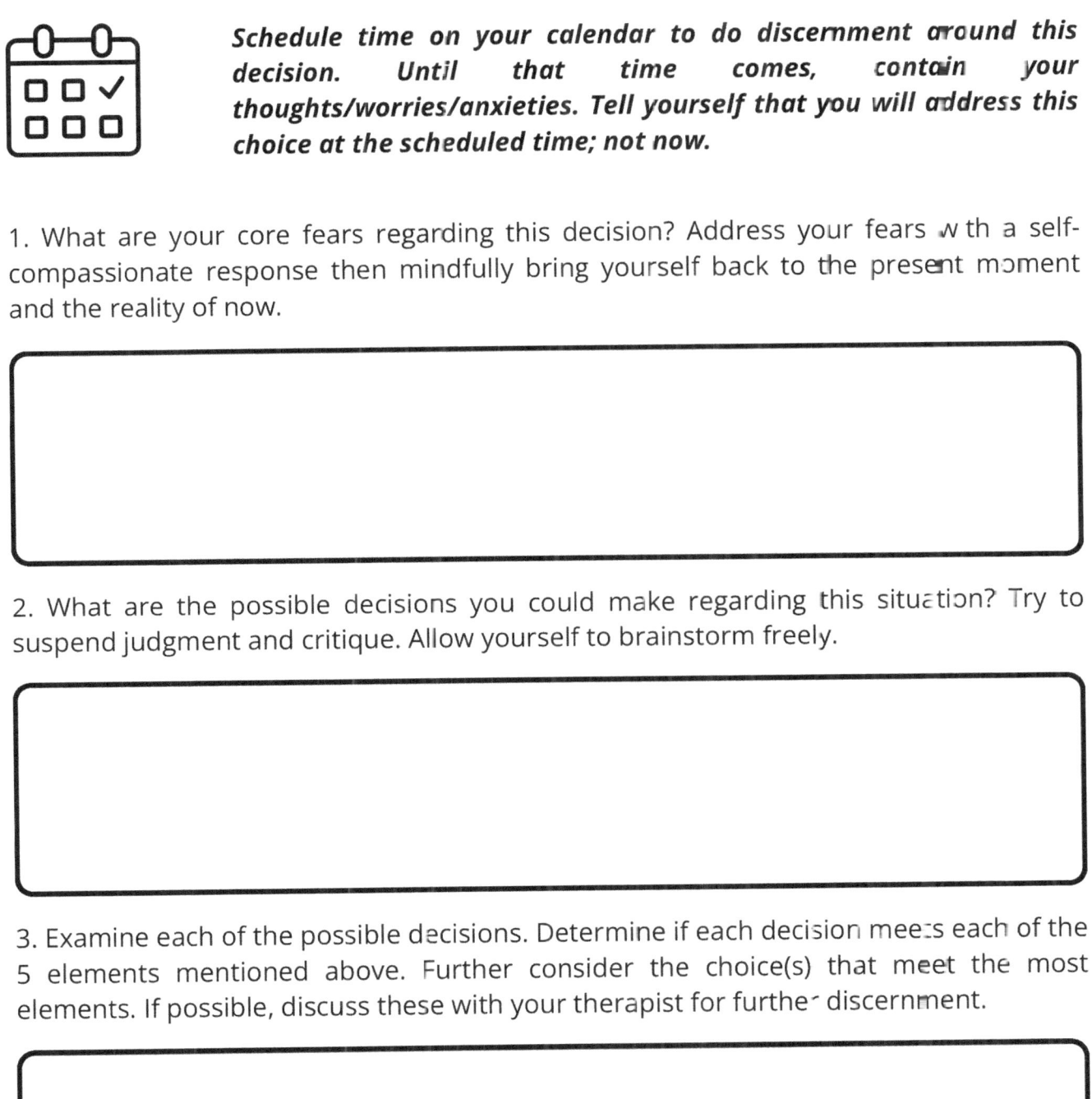

Schedule time on your calendar to do discernment around this decision. Until that time comes, contain your thoughts/worries/anxieties. Tell yourself that you will address this choice at the scheduled time; not now.

1. What are your core fears regarding this decision? Address your fears with a self-compassionate response then mindfully bring yourself back to the present moment and the reality of now.

2. What are the possible decisions you could make regarding this situation? Try to suspend judgment and critique. Allow yourself to brainstorm freely.

3. Examine each of the possible decisions. Determine if each decision meets each of the 5 elements mentioned above. Further consider the choice(s) that meet the most elements. If possible, discuss these with your therapist for further discernment.

Therapy Journal

*"Although the world is full of suffering,
it is also full of the overcoming of it."*
-Helen Keller

Therapy Journal

Date:

Location:

Name of Therapist:

Goal(s) for this session:

Topics discussed:

Insight / Things to remember:

Methods used during session:

Highlight the methods that were effective and helpful.

Homework / Next Steps:

Topics for next session:

Therapy Journal

Notes:

_____

_____

_____

_____

_____

_____

_____

_____

_____

_____

_____

_____

_____

_____

_____

_____

_____

_____

_____

_____

_____

_____

_____

_____

_____

Therapy Journal

Date: _____   **Location:** _____

Name of Therapist: _____

Goal(s) for this session: _____

Topics discussed: _____

Insight / Things to remember: _____

Methods used during session: _____

Highlight the methods that were effective and helpful.

Homework / Next Steps: _____

Topics for next session: _____

Therapy Journal

Notes:

_____

_____

_____

_____

_____

_____

_____

_____

_____

_____

_____

_____

_____

_____

_____

_____

_____

_____

_____

_____

_____

_____

_____

_____

_____

Therapy Journal

Date: [ ] **Location:** [ ]

Name of Therapist: [ ]

Goal(s) for this session: [ ]

Topics discussed: [ ]

Insight / Things to remember: [ ]

Methods used during session: [ ]

Highlight the methods that were effective and helpful.

Homework / Next Steps: [ ]

Topics for next session: [ ]

Therapy Journal

Notes:

_____

_____

_____

_____

_____

_____

_____

_____

_____

_____

_____

_____

_____

_____

_____

_____

_____

_____

_____

_____

_____

_____

_____

_____

_____

Therapy Journal

Date: [ ]   **Location:** [ ]

Name of Therapist: [ ]

Goal(s) for this session: [ ]

Topics discussed: [ ]

Insight / Things to remember: [ ]

Methods used during session: [ ]

Highlight the methods that were effective and helpful.

Homework / Next Steps: [ ]

Topics for next session: [ ]

Therapy Journal

Notes:

_____
_____
_____
_____
_____
_____
_____
_____
_____
_____
_____
_____
_____
_____
_____
_____
_____
_____
_____
_____
_____
_____
_____
_____

Therapy Journal

Date: _____   **Location:** _____

Name of Therapist: _____

Goal(s) for this session:

Topics discussed:

Insight / Things to remember:

Methods used during session:

Highlight the methods that were effective and helpful.

Homework / Next Steps:

Topics for next session:

Therapy Journal

Notes:

_____

_____

_____

_____

_____

_____

_____

_____

_____

_____

_____

_____

_____

_____

_____

_____

_____

_____

_____

_____

_____

_____

_____

_____

Therapy Journal

Date: _____   **Location:** _____

Name of Therapist: _____

Goal(s) for this session: _____

Topics discussed: _____

Insight / Things to remember: _____

Methods used during session: _____

Highlight the methods that were effective and helpful.

Homework / Next Steps: _____

Topics for next session: _____

Therapy Journal

Notes:

_____
_____
_____
_____
_____
_____
_____
_____
_____
_____
_____
_____
_____
_____
_____
_____
_____
_____
_____
_____
_____
_____
_____
_____
_____

Therapy Journal

Date: [   ]   **Location:** [   ]

Name of Therapist: [   ]

Goal(s) for this session:

Topics discussed:

Insight / Things to remember:

Methods used during session:

Highlight the methods that were effective and helpful.

Homework / Next Steps:

Topics for next session:

Therapy Journal

Notes:

_____

_____

_____

_____

_____

_____

_____

_____

_____

_____

_____

_____

_____

_____

_____

_____

_____

_____

_____

_____

_____

_____

_____

_____

_____

_____

_____

Therapy Journal

Date: [ ] **Location:** [ ]

Name of Therapist: [ ]

Goal(s) for this session:

Topics discussed:

Insight / Things to remember:

Methods used during session:

Highlight the methods that were effective and helpful.

Homework / Next Steps:

Topics for next session:

Therapy Journal

Notes:

_____

_____

_____

_____

_____

_____

_____

_____

_____

_____

_____

_____

_____

_____

_____

_____

_____

_____

_____

_____

_____

_____

_____

_____

_____

Therapy Journal

Date: [   ]   **Location:** [   ]

Name of Therapist: [   ]

Goal(s) for this session: [   ]

Topics discussed: [   ]

Insight / Things to remember: [   ]

Methods used during session: [   ]   *Highlight the methods that were effective and helpful.*

Homework / Next Steps: [   ]

Topics for next session: [   ]

Therapy Journal

Notes:

_____

_____

_____

_____

_____

_____

_____

_____

_____

_____

_____

_____

_____

_____

_____

_____

_____

_____

_____

_____

_____

_____

_____

_____

_____

Therapy Journal

Date: [   ] **Location:** [   ]

Name of Therapist: [   ]

Goal(s) for this session: [   ]

Topics discussed: [   ]

Insight / Things to remember: [   ]

Methods used during session: [   ]

Highlight the methods that were effective and helpful.

Homework / Next Steps: [   ]

Topics for next session: [   ]

Therapy Journal

Notes:

_____

_____

_____

_____

_____

_____

_____

_____

_____

_____

_____

_____

_____

_____

_____

_____

_____

_____

_____

_____

_____

_____

_____

_____

Therapy Journal

Date: _____ **Location:** _____

Name of Therapist: _____

Goal(s) for this session:

Topics discussed:

Insight / Things to remember:

Methods used during session:

Highlight the methods that were effective and helpful.

Homework / Next Steps:

Topics for next session:

Therapy Journal

Notes:

_____
_____
_____
_____
_____
_____
_____
_____
_____
_____
_____
_____
_____
_____
_____
_____
_____
_____
_____
_____
_____
_____
_____
_____

Therapy Journal

Date: _____ **Location:** _____

Name of Therapist: _____

Goal(s) for this session:

Topics discussed:

Insight / Things to remember:

Methods used during session:

Highlight the methods that were effective and helpful.

Homework / Next Steps:

Topics for next session:

Therapy Journal

Notes:

_____

_____

_____

_____

_____

_____

_____

_____

_____

_____

_____

_____

_____

_____

_____

_____

_____

_____

_____

_____

_____

_____

_____

_____

Therapy Journal

Date: [ ] **Location:** [ ]

Name of Therapist: [ ]

Goal(s) for this session: [ ]

Topics discussed: [ ]

Insight / Things to remember: [ ]

Methods used during session: [ ]

Highlight the methods that were effective and helpful.

Homework / Next Steps: [ ]

Topics for next session: [ ]

Therapy Journal

Notes:

_____

_____

_____

_____

_____

_____

_____

_____

_____

_____

_____

_____

_____

_____

_____

_____

_____

_____

_____

_____

_____

_____

_____

Therapy Journal

Date: [ ] **Location:** [ ]

Name of Therapist: [ ]

Goal(s) for this session: [ ]

Topics discussed: [ ]

Insight / Things to remember: [ ]

Methods used during session: [ ]

Highlight the methods that were effective and helpful.

Homework / Next Steps: [ ]

Topics for next session: [ ]

Therapy Journal

Notes:

_____

_____

_____

_____

_____

_____

_____

_____

_____

_____

_____

_____

_____

_____

_____

_____

_____

_____

_____

_____

_____

_____

_____

_____

_____

Therapy Journal

Date:

Location:

Name of Therapist:

Goal(s) for this session:

Topics discussed:

Insight / Things to remember:

Methods used during session:

Highlight the methods that were effective and helpful.

Homework / Next Steps:

Topics for next session:

Therapy Journal

Notes:

_____
_____
_____
_____
_____
_____
_____
_____
_____
_____
_____
_____
_____
_____
_____
_____
_____
_____
_____
_____
_____
_____
_____
_____

Therapy Journal

Date: [   ]   **Location:** [   ]

Name of Therapist: [   ]

Goal(s) for this session: [   ]

Topics discussed: [   ]

Insight / Things to remember: [   ]

Methods used during session: [   ]

Highlight the methods that were effective and helpful.

Homework / Next Steps: [   ]

Topics for next session: [   ]

Therapy Journal

Notes:

_____

_____

_____

_____

_____

_____

_____

_____

_____

_____

_____

_____

_____

_____

_____

_____

_____

_____

_____

_____

_____

_____

_____

_____

_____

Therapy Journal

Date:

Location:

Name of Therapist:

Goal(s) for this session:

Topics discussed:

Insight / Things to remember:

Methods used during session:

Highlight the methods that were effective and helpful.

Homework / Next Steps:

Topics for next session:

Therapy Journal

Notes:

_____

_____

_____

_____

_____

_____

_____

_____

_____

_____

_____

_____

_____

_____

_____

_____

_____

_____

_____

_____

_____

_____

_____

_____

_____

_____

Therapy Journal

Date: _____   **Location:** _____

Name of Therapist: _____

Goal(s) for this session:

Topics discussed:

Insight / Things to remember:

Methods used during session:

Highlight the methods that were effective and helpful.

Homework / Next Steps:

Topics for next session:

Therapy Journal

Notes:

_____

_____

_____

_____

_____

_____

_____

_____

_____

_____

_____

_____

_____

_____

_____

_____

_____

_____

_____

_____

_____

_____

_____

_____

_____

Therapy Journal

Date: _____ **Location:** _____

Name of Therapist: _____

Goal(s) for this
session:

Topics
discussed:

Insight / Things
to remember:

Methods used
during
session:

*Highlight the
methods that
were effective
and helpful.*

Homework /
Next Steps:

Topics for next
session:

Therapy Journal

Notes:

_____

_____

_____

_____

_____

_____

_____

_____

_____

_____

_____

_____

_____

_____

_____

_____

_____

_____

_____

_____

_____

_____

_____

_____

Therapy Journal

Date:

Location:

Name of Therapist:

Goal(s) for this session:

Topics discussed:

Insight / Things to remember:

Methods used during session:

Highlight the methods that were effective and helpful.

Homework / Next Steps:

Topics for next session:

Therapy Journal

Notes:

_____

_____

_____

_____

_____

_____

_____

_____

_____

_____

_____

_____

_____

_____

_____

_____

_____

_____

_____

_____

_____

_____

_____

_____

Therapy Journal

Date: [ ] **Location:** [ ]

Name of Therapist: [ ]

Goal(s) for this session: [ ]

Topics discussed: [ ]

Insight / Things to remember: [ ]

Methods used during session: [ ]

Highlight the methods that were effective and helpful.

Homework / Next Steps: [ ]

Topics for next session: [ ]

Therapy Journal

Notes:

_____

_____

_____

_____

_____

_____

_____

_____

_____

_____

_____

_____

_____

_____

_____

_____

_____

_____

_____

_____

_____

_____

_____

_____

Therapy Journal

Date: [   ]   **Location:** [   ]

Name of Therapist: [   ]

Goal(s) for this session:
[   ]

Topics discussed:
[   ]

Insight / Things to remember:
[   ]

Methods used during session:
[   ]

Highlight the methods that were effective and helpful.

Homework / Next Steps:
[   ]

Topics for next session:
[   ]

Therapy Journal

Notes:

_____
_____
_____
_____
_____
_____
_____
_____
_____
_____
_____
_____
_____
_____
_____
_____
_____
_____
_____
_____
_____
_____
_____
_____
_____

Therapy Journal

Date: [   ]   **Location:** [   ]

Name of Therapist: [   ]

Goal(s) for this session:

Topics discussed:

Insight / Things to remember:

Methods used during session:

Highlight the methods that were effective and helpful.

Homework / Next Steps:

Topics for next session:

Therapy Journal

Notes:

_____

_____

_____

_____

_____

_____

_____

_____

_____

_____

_____

_____

_____

_____

_____

_____

_____

_____

_____

_____

_____

_____

_____

_____

Therapy Journal

Date: [   ]   **Location:** [   ]

Name of Therapist: [   ]

Goal(s) for this session: [   ]

Topics discussed: [   ]

Insight / Things to remember: [   ]

Methods used during session: [   ]   *Highlight the methods that were effective and helpful.*

Homework / Next Steps: [   ]

Topics for next session: [   ]

Therapy Journal

Notes:

_____

_____

_____

_____

_____

_____

_____

_____

_____

_____

_____

_____

_____

_____

_____

_____

_____

_____

_____

_____

_____

_____

_____

_____

Therapy Journal

Date: [   ] **Location:** [   ]

Name of Therapist: [   ]

Goal(s) for this session:

Topics discussed:

Insight / Things to remember:

Methods used during session:

Highlight the methods that were effective and helpful.

Homework / Next Steps:

Topics for next session:

Therapy Journal

Notes:

_____
_____
_____
_____
_____
_____
_____
_____
_____
_____
_____
_____
_____
_____
_____
_____
_____
_____
_____
_____
_____
_____
_____
_____
_____
_____

Therapy Journal

Date: [_____]   **Location:** [_____]

Name of Therapist: [_____]

Goal(s) for this session: [_____]

Topics discussed: [_____]

Insight / Things to remember: [_____]

Methods used during session: [_____]

Highlight the methods that were effective and helpful.

Homework / Next Steps: [_____]

Topics for next session: [_____]

Therapy Journal

Notes:

_____

_____

_____

_____

_____

_____

_____

_____

_____

_____

_____

_____

_____

_____

_____

_____

_____

_____

_____

_____

_____

_____

_____

_____

Therapy Journal

Date: [   ]   **Location:** [   ]

Name of Therapist: [   ]

Goal(s) for this session:

Topics discussed:

Insight / Things to remember:

Methods used during session:

Highlight the methods that were effective and helpful.

Homework / Next Steps:

Topics for next session:

Therapy Journal

Notes:

_____

_____

_____

_____

_____

_____

_____

_____

_____

_____

_____

_____

_____

_____

_____

_____

_____

_____

_____

_____

_____

_____

_____

_____

_____

Therapy Journal

Date: _____ **Location:** _____

Name of Therapist: _____

Goal(s) for this session: _____

Topics discussed: _____

Insight / Things to remember: _____

Methods used during session: _____

Highlight the methods that were effective and helpful.

Homework / Next Steps: _____

Topics for next session: _____

Therapy Journal

Notes:

_____

_____

_____

_____

_____

_____

_____

_____

_____

_____

_____

_____

_____

_____

_____

_____

_____

_____

_____

_____

_____

_____

_____

_____

_____

Therapy Journal

Date: | **Location:**

Name of Therapist:

Goal(s) for this session:

Topics discussed:

Insight / Things to remember:

Methods used during session:

Highlight the methods that were effective and helpful.

Homework / Next Steps:

Topics for next session:

Therapy Journal

Notes:

_____

_____

_____

_____

_____

_____

_____

_____

_____

_____

_____

_____

_____

_____

_____

_____

_____

_____

_____

_____

_____

_____

_____

_____

_____

Therapy Journal

Date: [ ] **Location:** [ ]

Name of Therapist: [ ]

Goal(s) for this session:

Topics discussed:

Insight / Things to remember:

Methods used during session:

Highlight the methods that were effective and helpful.

Homework / Next Steps:

Topics for next session:

Therapy Journal

Notes:

_____

_____

_____

_____

_____

_____

_____

_____

_____

_____

_____

_____

_____

_____

_____

_____

_____

_____

_____

_____

_____

_____

_____

_____

_____

_____

_____

Therapy Journal

Date: [ ]   **Location:** [ ]

Name of Therapist: [ ]

Goal(s) for this session: [ ]

Topics discussed: [ ]

Insight / Things to remember: [ ]

Methods used during session: [ ]

Highlight the methods that were effective and helpful.

Homework / Next Steps: [ ]

Topics for next session: [ ]

Therapy Journal

Notes:

_____
_____
_____
_____
_____
_____
_____
_____
_____
_____
_____
_____
_____
_____
_____
_____
_____
_____
_____
_____
_____
_____
_____
_____
_____
_____
_____

Therapy Journal

Date: [_____] **Location:** [_____]

Name of Therapist: [_____]

Goal(s) for this session: [_____]

Topics discussed: [_____]

Insight / Things to remember: [_____]

Methods used during session: [_____]

Highlight the methods that were effective and helpful.

Homework / Next Steps: [_____]

Topics for next session: [_____]

Therapy Journal

Notes:

_____
_____
_____
_____
_____
_____
_____
_____
_____
_____
_____
_____
_____
_____
_____
_____
_____
_____
_____
_____
_____
_____
_____
_____
_____

Therapy Journal

Date: [ ] **Location:** [ ]

Name of Therapist: [ ]

Goal(s) for this session: [ ]

Topics discussed: [ ]

Insight / Things to remember: [ ]

Methods used during session: [ ]

Highlight the methods that were effective and helpful.

Homework / Next Steps: [ ]

Topics for next session: [ ]

Therapy Journal

Notes:

_____

_____

_____

_____

_____

_____

_____

_____

_____

_____

_____

_____

_____

_____

_____

_____

_____

_____

_____

_____

_____

_____

_____

_____

_____

Therapy Journal

Date: _____ **Location:** _____

Name of Therapist: _____

Goal(s) for this session: _____

Topics discussed: _____

Insight / Things to remember: _____

Methods used during session: _____

Highlight the methods that were effective and helpful.

Homework / Next Steps: _____

Topics for next session: _____

Therapy Journal

Notes:

_____
_____
_____
_____
_____
_____
_____
_____
_____
_____
_____
_____
_____
_____
_____
_____
_____
_____
_____
_____
_____
_____
_____
_____

Therapy Journal

Date: _____   **Location:** _____

Name of Therapist: _____

Goal(s) for this session:

Topics discussed:

Insight / Things to remember:

Methods used during session:

Highlight the methods that were effective and helpful.

Homework / Next Steps:

Topics for next session:

Therapy Journal

Notes:

_____
_____
_____
_____
_____
_____
_____
_____
_____
_____
_____
_____
_____
_____
_____
_____
_____
_____
_____
_____
_____
_____
_____
_____
_____

Therapy Journal

Date: _____   **Location:** _____

Name of Therapist: _____

Goal(s) for this session: _____

Topics discussed: _____

Insight / Things to remember: _____

Methods used during session: _____

Highlight the methods that were effective and helpful.

Homework / Next Steps: _____

Topics for next session: _____

Therapy Journal

Notes:

_____

_____

_____

_____

_____

_____

_____

_____

_____

_____

_____

_____

_____

_____

_____

_____

_____

_____

_____

_____

_____

_____

_____

_____

Therapy Journal

Date: [ ] **Location:** [ ]

Name of Therapist: [ ]

Goal(s) for this session:

Topics discussed:

Insight / Things to remember:

Methods used during session:

Highlight the methods that were effective and helpful.

Homework / Next Steps:

Topics for next session:

Therapy Journal

Notes:

_____

_____

_____

_____

_____

_____

_____

_____

_____

_____

_____

_____

_____

_____

_____

_____

_____

_____

_____

_____

_____

_____

_____

_____

_____

Therapy Journal

Date: _____   **Location:** _____

Name of Therapist: _____

Goal(s) for this session:

Topics discussed:

Insight / Things to remember:

Methods used during session:

Highlight the methods that were effective and helpful.

Homework / Next Steps:

Topics for next session:

Therapy Journal

Notes:

_____
_____
_____
_____
_____
_____
_____
_____
_____
_____
_____
_____
_____
_____
_____
_____
_____
_____
_____
_____
_____
_____
_____
_____
_____

Therapy Journal

Date: [ ] **Location:** [ ]

Name of Therapist: [ ]

Goal(s) for this session: [ ]

Topics discussed: [ ]

Insight / Things to remember: [ ]

Methods used during session: [ ]

Highlight the methods that were effective and helpful.

Homework / Next Steps: [ ]

Topics for next session: [ ]

Therapy Journal

Notes:

_____

_____

_____

_____

_____

_____

_____

_____

_____

_____

_____

_____

_____

_____

_____

_____

_____

_____

_____

_____

_____

_____

_____

_____

_____

_____

Therapy Journal

Date: _____   **Location:** _____

Name of Therapist: _____

Goal(s) for this session:

Topics discussed:

Insight / Things to remember:

Methods used during session:

Highlight the methods that were effective and helpful.

Homework / Next Steps:

Topics for next session:

Therapy Journal

Notes:

_____

_____

_____

_____

_____

_____

_____

_____

_____

_____

_____

_____

_____

_____

_____

_____

_____

_____

_____

_____

_____

_____

_____

_____

Therapy Journal

Date: [   ]   **Location:** [   ]

Name of Therapist: [   ]

Goal(s) for this session:

Topics discussed:

Insight / Things to remember:

Methods used during session:

Highlight the methods that were effective and helpful.

Homework / Next Steps:

Topics for next session:

Therapy Journal

Notes:

_____
_____
_____
_____
_____
_____
_____
_____
_____
_____
_____
_____
_____
_____
_____
_____
_____
_____
_____
_____
_____
_____
_____
_____
_____
_____

Therapy Journal

Date: _____   **Location:** _____

Name of Therapist: _____

Goal(s) for this session:

Topics discussed:

Insight / Things to remember:

Methods used during session:

Highlight the methods that were effective and helpful.

Homework / Next Steps:

Topics for next session:

Therapy Journal

Notes:

_____

_____

_____

_____

_____

_____

_____

_____

_____

_____

_____

_____

_____

_____

_____

_____

_____

_____

_____

_____

_____

_____

_____

_____

_____

Therapy Journal

Date:

Location:

Name of Therapist:

Goal(s) for this session:

Topics discussed:

Insight / Things to remember:

Methods used during session:

Highlight the methods that were effective and helpful.

Homework / Next Steps:

Topics for next session:

Therapy Journal

Notes:

_____

_____

_____

_____

_____

_____

_____

_____

_____

_____

_____

_____

_____

_____

_____

_____

_____

_____

_____

_____

_____

_____

_____

_____

Therapy Journal

Date: _____   **Location:** _____

Name of Therapist: _____

Goal(s) for this session:

Topics discussed:

Insight / Things to remember:

Methods used during session:

Highlight the methods that were effective and helpful.

Homework / Next Steps:

Topics for next session:

Therapy Journal

Notes:

_____

_____

_____

_____

_____

_____

_____

_____

_____

_____

_____

_____

_____

_____

_____

_____

_____

_____

_____

_____

_____

_____

_____

_____

_____

Therapy Journal

Date: _____   **Location:** _____

Name of Therapist: _____

Goal(s) for this session:

Topics discussed:

Insight / Things to remember:

Methods used during session:

Highlight the methods that were effective and helpful.

Homework / Next Steps:

Topics for next session:

Therapy Journal

Notes:

_____

_____

_____

_____

_____

_____

_____

_____

_____

_____

_____

_____

_____

_____

_____

_____

_____

_____

_____

_____

_____

_____

_____

_____

_____

Therapy Journal

Date: [   ] **Location:** [   ]

Name of Therapist: [   ]

Goal(s) for this session: [   ]

Topics discussed: [   ]

Insight / Things to remember: [   ]

Methods used during session: [   ] *Highlight the methods that were effective and helpful.*

Homework / Next Steps: [   ]

Topics for next session: [   ]

Therapy Journal

Notes:

_____

_____

_____

_____

_____

_____

_____

_____

_____

_____

_____

_____

_____

_____

_____

_____

_____

_____

_____

_____

_____

_____

_____

_____

_____

Therapy Journal

Date: [ ]   Location: [ ]

Name of Therapist: [ ]

Goal(s) for this session: [ ]

Topics discussed: [ ]

Insight / Things to remember: [ ]

Methods used during session: [ ]

Highlight the methods that were effective and helpful.

Homework / Next Steps: [ ]

Topics for next session: [ ]

Therapy Journal

Notes:

_____
_____
_____
_____
_____
_____
_____
_____
_____
_____
_____
_____
_____
_____
_____
_____
_____
_____
_____
_____
_____
_____
_____
_____
_____
_____
_____

Therapy Journal

Date: [   ] Location: [   ]

Name of Therapist: [   ]

Goal(s) for this session:

Topics discussed:

Insight / Things to remember:

Methods used during session:

Highlight the methods that were effective and helpful.

Homework / Next Steps:

Topics for next session:

Therapy Journal

Notes:

_____

_____

_____

_____

_____

_____

_____

_____

_____

_____

_____

_____

_____

_____

_____

_____

_____

_____

_____

_____

_____

_____

_____

_____

_____

Therapy Journal

Date: [   ]   **Location:** [   ]

Name of Therapist: [   ]

Goal(s) for this session:

Topics discussed:

Insight / Things to remember:

Methods used during session:

Highlight the methods that were effective and helpful.

Homework / Next Steps:

Topics for next session:

Therapy Journal

Notes:

_____
_____
_____
_____
_____
_____
_____
_____
_____
_____
_____
_____
_____
_____
_____
_____
_____
_____
_____
_____
_____
_____
_____
_____
_____
_____

Therapy Journal

Date: [ ] **Location:** [ ]

Name of Therapist: [ ]

Goal(s) for this session: [ ]

Topics discussed: [ ]

Insight / Things to remember: [ ]

Methods used during session: [ ]

Highlight the methods that were effective and helpful.

Homework / Next Steps: [ ]

Topics for next session: [ ]

Therapy Journal

Notes:

_____

_____

_____

_____

_____

_____

_____

_____

_____

_____

_____

_____

_____

_____

_____

_____

_____

_____

_____

_____

_____

_____

_____

_____

Therapy Journal

Date: [ ]   **Location:** [ ]

Name of Therapist: [ ]

Goal(s) for this session: [ ]

Topics discussed: [ ]

Insight / Things to remember: [ ]

Methods used during session: [ ]

Highlight the methods that were effective and helpful.

Homework / Next Steps: [ ]

Topics for next session: [ ]

Therapy Journal

Notes:

_____

_____

_____

_____

_____

_____

_____

_____

_____

_____

_____

_____

_____

_____

_____

_____

_____

_____

_____

_____

_____

_____

_____

_____

Therapy Journal

Date: [   ]　　**Location:** [   ]

Name of Therapist: [   ]

Goal(s) for this session: [   ]

Topics discussed: [   ]

Insight / Things to remember: [   ]

Methods used during session: [   ]

Highlight the methods that were effective and helpful.

Homework / Next Steps: [   ]

Topics for next session: [   ]

Therapy Journal

Notes:

_____

_____

_____

_____

_____

_____

_____

_____

_____

_____

_____

_____

_____

_____

_____

_____

_____

_____

_____

_____

_____

_____

_____

Therapy Journal

Date: **Location:**

Name of Therapist:

Goal(s) for this session:

Topics discussed:

Insight / Things to remember:

Methods used during session:

Highlight the methods that were effective and helpful.

Homework / Next Steps:

Topics for next session:

Therapy Journal

Notes:

_____

_____

_____

_____

_____

_____

_____

_____

_____

_____

_____

_____

_____

_____

_____

_____

_____

_____

_____

_____

_____

_____

_____

_____

_____

www.ingramcontent.com/pod-product-compliance
Lightning Source LLC
Chambersburg PA
CBHW080841120626
46553CB00009B/2520